WHAT DO YOU DO IF YOU WORK AT THE

ZOO?

STEVE JENKINS AND ROBIN PAGE

HOUGHTON MIFFLIN HARCOURT   BOSTON • NEW YORK

What do you do if you work at the zoo?

Y ou'll be a zookeeper—a person who takes care of the animals. You'll feed your animals, of course. And you'll do your best to make sure they stay healthy and safe. But zookeepers also have more unusual responsibilities. You might find yourself playing games with a monkey, imitating a vulture, weighing a snake—even tickling a tapir.

Here are a few of the surprising things *you* might do if you decide to work at the zoo.

Cuddle a joey

A mother kangaroo keeps her baby—called a joey—safe in a pouch on her belly. This joey doesn't have a mother, so for the next six months you'll carry it in your own pouch made of cloth.

Impersonate a vulture

This king vulture chick is being raised in a zoo, but when it is old enough it will be released into the wild. To keep it from becoming attached to a human, you should feed it with a hand puppet that looks like an adult vulture.

Count a colony

It's important to keep track of all the animals in a zoo. Making a regular count of these Humboldt penguins will ensure that none of them are missing or sick.

Rub an aardvark's ears

At home in Africa, aardvarks are nighttime creatures. But in a zoo they are often active during the day. You'll need to slather sunscreen onto the aardvark's sensitive ears to keep them from getting sunburned.

Shine a tortoise's shell

Polishing this Galápagos tortoise's shell keeps it from drying out and cracking. And the tortoise seems to enjoy the attention.

An elephant living in the zoo doesn't walk miles every day like its wild cousins, so its toenails don't get worn down. This elephant is trained to hold up its feet one at a time so you can file down its toenails.

Give an elephant a pedicure

A wild hippopotamus feeds on grass and water plants that don't get stuck in its teeth. But the fruits and vegetables it eats in the zoo can get trapped and give the hippo cavities, so you'll need to give its huge tusks a regular brushing.

Brush a hippo's teeth

Puzzle a meerkat . . .

Why hide a meerkat's snack? It's not always easy for a wild animal to find food. When you give this meerkat a puzzle—it must figure out which tube has a treat inside—you'll be encouraging its natural behavior.

...then warm it up

In Africa, meerkats like to bask in the sun. When it's cold outside, you can help them stay toasty by turning on an infrared heat lamp.

Serenade a seal

If you're a musician, try playing a tune for a seal. The music seems to calm it down.

Tickle a tapir

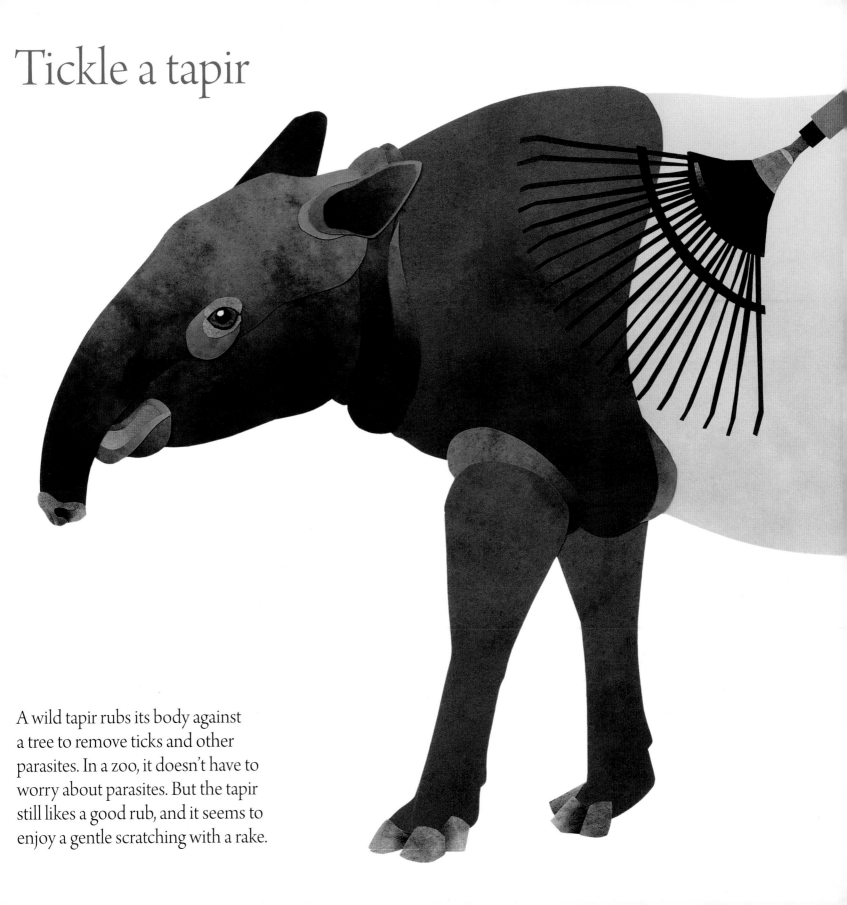

A wild tapir rubs its body against a tree to remove ticks and other parasites. In a zoo, it doesn't have to worry about parasites. But the tapir still likes a good rub, and it seems to enjoy a gentle scratching with a rake.

Play ball with a bear …

Playtime is an important part of the day for many animals. It keeps them entertained—and it's good exercise. Try tossing a ball to this polar bear. She'll love it, but you might not get your ball back right away.

… and pass to a rhino

How about playing soccer with a rhinoceros? Make the pass, then get out of the way—fast.

Train a dragon

How do you get a dangerous giant lizard to climb into its cage so a vet can give it a checkup? Train it to pursue a red ball on a stick to get a reward. When the Komodo dragon follows the ball into its cage, give it a dead rat—what a treat!

Pick up panda poop

Pandas eat almost nothing but bamboo. And they eat a lot of it. Which means they make a lot of poop. So get your shovel. It's a dirty job, but somebody has to do it. And not just for the pandas—zookeepers clean up after all the animals in the zoo.

Don't make this at home

When it's hot, kids aren't the only ones that like Popsicles. Zoo animals get fruitsicles, fishsicles, and meatsicles. You can make a hyena happy with a bloodsicle.

Bottle-feed a giraffe...

This little giraffe's mother is sick and can't nurse her baby, so you'll need to give the calf a bottle of milk every few hours. It just might decide that *you're* its mother.

... or a manatee

A hurricane separated this baby manatee from its mother. Manatees are mammals, and their young drink milk. You'll be feeding it by hand for the next year or so.

Size up a guitarfish

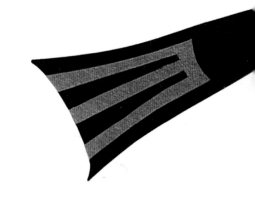

If you know how to scuba dive, you can measure this guitarfish—a close relative of the shark. Keeping track of an animal's size lets you know if it's healthy and growing properly.

Pick up a python

Keeping track of an animal's weight is one way to make sure it is getting enough food. But to weigh a 350-pound (160-kilogram) snake, you'll need to recruit some friends.

Entice an elephant seal

How do you weigh an elephant seal? This enormous animal is happy to flop onto a scale as long as you reward it with lots of yummy raw fish.

Introduce a friend

Cheetah cubs usually have several brothers and sisters. But this cheetah was born alone, and it seems to be lonely. Try introducing it to a new playmate: a golden retriever puppy.

What does a zookeeper do?

A zookeeper's responsibilities vary, but here are a few things that are often part of the job:

• Regularly check on the animals they are responsible for to make sure none of them are sick or injured.

• Make sure their animals are getting the right kinds and amounts of food and medicine.

• Keep each animal's enclosure clean and safe.

• Stimulate the animals and encourage them to use their natural behaviors by playing games with them, giving them puzzles to solve, offering them food in new ways, or introducing new objects to their habitat.

• Train animals to remain motionless, hold out a foot or other body part, or open their mouth so that zoo veterinarians and dentists can treat them.

• Educate visitors by answering questions or giving talks.

Zoo pros and cons

Some people argue that it's wrong to keep wild animals captive, even if they are well cared for. Many others believe that the benefits of zoos outweigh the animals' loss of freedom. It's difficult to know what animals are thinking and feeling, but the fact is that life in the wild can be harsh. Sickness, predators, parasites, and human poachers are risks that animals face in their natural habitats. Zoo animals are kept well fed and as healthy as possible.

Modern scientific zoos have three main missions:

Education
Seeing an animal such as a tiger or rhinoceros up close is different from learning about it in a book or on a TV show. The experience can make people more aware of the threats wild animals face and more concerned about protecting them.

Research
By studying the animals in a zoo, scientists can learn how to help their wild relatives survive the threats of human development, climate change, and disease.

Conservation
Many animals that are endangered—or extinct—in the wild are raised in zoos and eventually reintroduced into their natural habitats.

A zoo timeline

Before zoos, there were menageries—collections of exotic animals kept by kings or wealthy people. The earliest menagerie we know of was in Egypt more than 5,000 years ago.

During the 1700s and 1800s, zoos were collections of animals put on view to entertain the public. The animals were often kept in small cages and treated poorly.

Some of the world's top zoos

There are more than one thousand zoos in the world, and they are not all the same. Here are a few of the zoos that are considered among the best in the world.

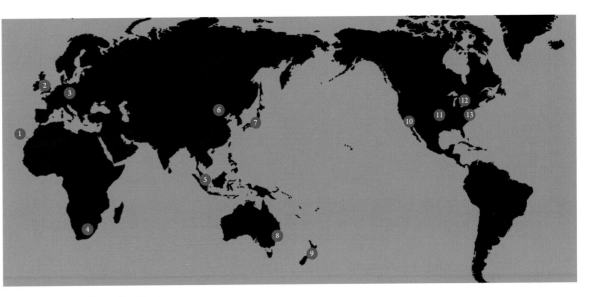

1 **Loro Parque** Tenerife, Spain
2 **London Zoo** London, England
3 **Berlin Zoo** Berlin, Germany
4 **Natural Zoological Gardens** Pretoria, South Africa
5 **Singapore Zoo** Singapore
6 **Beijing Zoo** Beijing, China
7 **Yokohama Zoological Gardens** Yokohama, Japan
8 **Sydney Zoo** Sydney, Australia
9 **Wellington Zoo** Wellington, New Zealand
10 **San Diego Zoo** San Diego, California (USA)
11 **Henry Doorly Zoo** Omaha, Nebraska (USA)
12 **Toronto Zoo** Toronto, Canada
13 **National Zoological Park** Washington, DC (USA)

About two hundred years ago, people started to think of zoos in a different way. Scientists began to study the behavior and anatomy of zoo animals, and their habitats were changed to more closely resemble their native environments.

In modern zoos, the well-being of the animals is the primary goal. These zoos create habitats and routines for their inhabitants that are as close as possible to what the animals would experience in the wild (without the dangers of predators, parasites, and starvation).

Red kangaroos live in eastern Australia, where they graze on grass and other plants. Kangaroos live in herds, known as *mobs*, of up to 50 animals. A full-grown male red kangaroo can stand taller than a man and leap 30 feet (9 meters) in a single bound. But a newborn baby kangaroo is tiny—about the size of a grape. As soon as it is born, it climbs into a pouch on its mother's belly and begins to nurse. At around four months of age, it begins to leave the pouch for short periods. It will move out completely at about ten months.

The **king vulture** is found in Central and South America. It is a scavenger, using its powerful beak to feed on the carcasses of dead animals. When full-grown, this large bird has a wingspan of up to seven feet (2 meters). The mother vulture lays a single egg, and both parents help raise the chick. The young bird grows quickly and is ready to fly when it is about three months old.

Humboldt penguins nest on the rocky Pacific coast of Peru and Chile in South America. These birds stand about two feet (61 centimeters) tall. They are fast and agile in the water, swimming at speeds of up to 30 miles per hour (48 kilometers per hour). They hunt fish, shrimp, and squid. Humboldt penguins are threatened by fishing and the loss of their habitat due to human activity.

As it roams the plains and forests of central and southern Africa, the **aardvark** sniffs out ant and termite colonies. It rips their nests open with powerful claws and slurps up thousands of insects with a sticky, foot-long (30-centimeters-long) tongue. The aardvark, whose name means "earth pig" in an African language, is active at night and sleeps in a burrow during the day. Including its tail, it can reach seven feet (more than 2 meters) in length.

The **Galápagos tortoise**, the largest tortoise in the world, is found only on the Galápagos Islands off the coast of Ecuador in the Pacific Ocean. It can weigh more than 500 pounds (227 kilograms) and live to be more than 170 years old. This gentle, slow-moving giant eats grass, cacti, and other plants. It can survive for up to a year without food or water.

The largest living land animal is the **African elephant**. An adult male can stand 10 feet (3 meters) tall at the shoulder and weigh 12,000 pounds (5,443 kilograms). An elephant may eat 600 pounds (272 kilograms) of roots, leaves, and fruit a day. African elephants live in grasslands and forests in central and southern Africa.

The lakes and rivers of central Africa are home to the **hippopotamus**, a plant-eating mammal that is a distant relative of the whales. Hippos spend the hot days submerged in the water. They come out at night to graze on grass and other plants. Male hippos protect their stretch of river with their huge mouths and long tusks. They are one of the world's most dangerous large animals, causing as many as 500 human deaths every year. The hippo is the second-largest land animal (after the elephant), weighing from 3,000 to 8,000 pounds (1,360 to 3,630 kilograms).

Meerkats live in the dry plains and deserts of southern Africa. They live in groups, or mobs, of up to 50 animals. They sleep in underground burrows at night and emerge to hunt for insects, birds' eggs, scorpions, and other small animals during the day. Meerkats are about 12 inches (30 centimeters) in length. They take turns standing on their back legs and watching for danger. The black fur around the meerkats' eyes helps reduce glare from the sun, making it easier for them to see approaching danger.

The **leopard seal** is also known as a sea leopard. As its name suggests, this seal is a predator. It hunts fish, squid, penguins, and other seals in the cold waters around Antarctica. It also feeds on small shrimplike animals called krill. Leopard seals are big. They reach 12 feet (3½ meters) in length and can weigh more than 800 pounds (363 kilograms). In their polar habitat, only the killer whale is bigger.

The **Malayan tapir** is found in the rainforests of Southeast Asia. It is an herbivore, eating grass, leaves, and water plants. A large male tapir can weigh more than 1,000 pounds (454 kilograms). The tapir's black-and-white coat acts as camouflage by breaking up the animal's silhouette as it moves through the light and shadows of the forest. Tapirs have poor eyesight but an excellent sense of smell, which they rely on to find food and warn them of predators.

A large **polar bear** can weigh as much as 1,600 pounds (726 kilograms). Along with the Kodiak brown bear, it is the world's largest carnivorous land animal. Polar bears live on the land and ice sheets surrounding the Arctic Ocean. They stalk and kill seals, and sometimes feed on the carcasses of dead whales and other animals. The polar bear has an excellent sense of smell. It can sniff out a seal hiding in its den beneath several feet of snow. Polar bears do most of their hunting on floating sea ice. A warming climate is melting much of this ice and will eventually threaten these bears with extinction.

Some people in Asia believe that the horn of the **black rhinoceros** has magical medical properties, and they are willing to pay enormous sums of money for a horn. Unfortunately, this has led to widespread poaching—illegal hunting—and the rhinoceros is now critically endangered. This large herbivore can weigh more than 3,000 pounds (1,361 kilograms). It feeds on plant leaves, twigs, shoots, and fruit. Black rhinos live in the forests and grasslands of eastern and southern Africa.

The largest lizard on earth, the **Komodo dragon**, is found on just a few islands in the southwest Pacific Ocean. It is a fierce predator, killing and eating deer, pigs, water buffalo, other Komodo dragons, and—rarely—humans. This big reptile can be 10 feet (3 meters) long and can weigh 300 pounds (136 kilograms). Its bite is venomous. When it attacks a large animal such as a buffalo, its bite injects a slow-acting poison. Using its excellent sense of smell, it follows its prey, sometimes for days, until the poison makes the animal too weak to escape. A Komodo dragon can consume almost its own weight in one meal.

The **giant panda**, with its distinctive black-and-white coat, is a well-known animal. But in the wild, it is found in just a few small mountainous regions of central China. It lives in forests of bamboo—the plants that make up almost all of its diet. Bamboo is not very nutritious, so pandas must eat a lot of it. An adult panda can weigh more than 300 pounds (136 kilograms) and eat 40 pounds (18 kilograms) of bamboo every day. This results in a lot of panda poop: these bears poop up to 40 times a day.

The **spotted hyena** is a powerful predator that hunts wildebeests, zebras, and antelopes. It will also eat carrion—dead animals—and almost any other animal it can catch, including fish, snakes, frogs, small mammals, and occasionally humans. The hyena resembles a large dog—it can weigh as much as 190 pounds (86 kilograms)—but it is more closely related to a cat. Hyenas are found throughout much of central and southern Africa.

A newborn **giraffe** is as tall as a full-grown man, and it can walk within hours of its birth. By the time it's an adult, it may reach 18 feet (5½ meters) in height—making it the tallest animal on land. Giraffes live on the plains and savannas of central and southern Africa, where they graze on leaves, grass, and fruit. They form groups—called *towers*—that can include dozens of animals.

The warm, shallow coastal waters of Florida, the Caribbean, and the Gulf of Mexico are home to the **West Indian manatee**. This gentle, plant-eating mammal, also known as a sea cow, spends most of its time moving through the water as it feeds on sea grass and other water plants. It uses its flippers to walk along the bottom and scoop up vegetation. Manatees are large animals, measuring up to 13 feet (4 meters) long and weighing 1,200 pounds (544 kilograms). Baby manatees are born underwater. Like all mammals, they breathe air, so the baby's mother pushes it to the surface to take its first breaths. A newborn manatee can weigh 60 pounds (27 kilograms).

The **shovelnose guitarfish**, a kind of ray, gets its name from its flat, guitar-shaped body and long, triangular snout. It lives on sandy seafloors off the Pacific coast of the United States and Mexico. This fish reaches five and a half feet (168 centimeters) in length. It is a bottom feeder, preying on crabs, clams, shrimp, and other seafloor animals. It ambushes its prey by burying itself in the sand with just its eyes sticking out. When a crab or other small creature gets close, the guitarfish lunges and grabs it.

At 33 feet (10 meters) in length, the **reticulated python** is the world's longest snake. That's a record—most of these snakes are shorter, averaging about 20 feet (6 meters) in length. This python lives in the jungles of Southeast Asia and hunts deer, pigs, monkeys, and other mammals. It is a constrictor. It grabs an animal with its sharp, backward-facing fangs, wraps its coil around its victim, and squeezes until it suffocates its prey. Then it swallows its victim whole.

The **southern elephant seal** lives in the cold ocean waters around Antarctica. These huge mammals can reach a weight of 9,000 pounds (4,082 kilograms). Elephant seals can dive to depths of 3,000 feet (914 meters) and hold their breath for two hours as they pursue the squid and fish that make up most of their diet. The elephant seal didn't get its name from its size, but from its trunk-like snout.

Over short distances, the **cheetah**—the world's fastest land animal—can sprint at more than 60 miles per hour (96 kilometers per hour). These speedy cats live in scattered habitats—mostly open forests and grasslands—throughout Africa. They are also found in one region of Iran, though there are only a few dozen of these Asian cheetahs left in the wild. Cheetahs use their speed to run down antelopes and smaller animals such as birds and hares. Cheetahs are usually born in litters of three to five cubs, and the siblings may hunt together throughout their lives.

For Page, Alec, and Jamie —S.J. and R.P.

Bibliography

Bruno Munari's Zoo. By Bruno Munari. Chronicle Books, 2005.

Life at the Zoo. By Michael George. Sterling Children's Books, 2018.

Life at the Zoo: Behind the Scenes with the Animal Doctors. By Phillip T. Robinson. Columbia University Press, 2004.

Lunch at the Zoo: What Animals Eat and Why. By Joyce Altman. Scholastic, 2001.

Should There Be Zoos?: A Persuasive Text. By Tony Stead. Mondo Pub, 2002.

Working at the Zoo (21st Century Junior Library: Careers). By Tamra B. Orr. Cherry Lake Publishing, 2013.

You Belong in a Zoo!: Tales from a Lifetime Spent with Cobras, Crocs, and Other Creatures. By Peter Brazaitis. Villard, 2003.

ZooBorns: The Next Generation: Newer, Cuter, More Exotic Animals from the World's Zoos and Aquariums. By Andrew Bleiman and Chris Eastland. Simon and Schuster, 2012.

Zoo Story: Life in the Garden of Captives. By Thomas French. Hyperion, 2010.

Text copyright © 2020 by Robin Page and Steve Jenkins
Illustrations copyright © 2020 by Steve Jenkins

hmhbooks.com

The illustrations in this book were done in cut- and torn-paper collage.
The text type was set in Armo Pro.
The display type was set in Futura.

Library of Congress Catalog Control Number 2019020334.

ISBN: 978-0-544-38759-1

Manufactured in China
SCP 10 9 8 7 6 5 4 3 2 1
4500789326